# Promoting recovery from first episode psychosis

# Promoting recovery from first episode psychosis

## A guide for families

Sabrina Baker, MSW, RSW

Lisa Martens, MSW, RSW

camh

Centre for Addiction and Mental Health
Centre de toxicomanie et de santé mentale

Library and Archives Canada Cataloguing in Publication

Baker, Sabrina
    Promoting recovery from first episode psychosis : a guide for families / Sabrina
Baker, Lisa Martens.

Issued also in PDF and ePub format.
ISBN 978-1-77052-382-1

    1. Psychoses.  2. Psychoses--Patients--Rehabilitation.
3. Psychoses--Patients--Family relationships.  4. Families of the mentally ill.  I. Martens,
Lisa  II. Title.

RC512.B34 2010              362.2'6          C2009-907504-0

ISBN: 978-1-77052-382-1 (PRINT)
ISBN: 978-1-77052-383-8 (PDF)
ISBN: 978-1-77052-384-5 (HTML)
ISBN: 978-1-77052-385-2 (ePUB)

Printed in Canada

Website: www.camh.net

This guide was produced by:
Development: Caroline Hebblethwaite, CAMH
Editorial: Jacquelyn Waller-Vintar, Kelly Coleman, CAMH
Design: Mara Korkola, CAMH
Cover art: "Cauldron sol et mew, she said" by David Humphreys, reproduced with
permission of the artist
Print production: Christine Harris, CAMH

4070 / 03-2010 / PM091

# Contents

# PART II: Promoting recovery for you, the family member

# Preface

The idea for creating this guide grew from the ongoing questions, observations, input, ideas and suggestions of families and other caregivers who have a loved one experiencing a first episode of psychosis.

Most young people who develop a first episode of psychosis live with their families or are dependent on their family in some way. As a family member, you can play a significant role in:

- helping to identify early signs of psychosis
- seeking prompt and appropriate treatment for your relative
- promoting the recovery process.

We recognize that the person who has experienced psychosis needs support. We also know that family members often need assistance with their own recovery process. The more informed and supported *you* are, the better the outcome for you and your relative.

## USING THIS GUIDE

The information in this guide is general, and may not always apply to every family member's situation. We encourage you to discuss your concerns and questions with the treatment team members.

This guide is based on research, practice guidelines and our own experience working with our clients and their families. We recognize that each family's situation is unique and that the availability of resources and treatment approaches will vary depending on where you live.

How you use this guide will depend on your learning style, how your loved one is doing and how long your family has been coping with a first episode of psychosis.

The guide is divided into two parts.

Part one, **Promoting recovery for your relative with psychosis**, is designed to assist you, the family member, in becoming an ally and participant in your relative's recovery. The focus is on your ill relative's needs and is recovery-based. This section provides hands-on practical advice about how to deal with psychosis, stay well and promote recovery for your relative.

Part two, **Promoting recovery for you, the family member,** is designed to help you to understand what you are going through as you help your relative recover. The focus is on the family's needs and is also recovery-based. Part two outlines specialized services for families, and offers practical suggestions for family members to nurture themselves, communicate more effectively and set limits.

# ACKNOWLEDGMENTS

We are indebted to the family members we work with. They have inspired us to write this manual and have demonstrated how much resilience, wisdom and expertise families have in coping with a relative who has experienced a first episode of psychosis.

Lisa, who was working with the First Episode Division (FED) as a social worker on 10 Early Psychosis Unit, was approached by Jean Addington to write this guide. She brought on board Sabrina, a social worker who specializes in family work who works at LEARN (Learning Employment Advocacy Recreation Network) at CAMH, and together we wrote this guide, draft after draft. Sabrina used this manual to train family workers and professionals, consult across Ontario, and conduct family workshops for organizations such as the Schizophrenia Society of Ontario and the Ontario Working Group for Early Intervention. This gave us more insight on how to make this manual useful and relevant for our families.

Rob Peach, a social worker on our Home Intervention Psychosis (HIP) team, regularly co-facilitates with Sabrina on Family Psychosis Education and Taking Care of the Caregiver groups at LEARN, further strengthening the guide's content with valuable feedback. Special thanks go to those families who permitted us to share their own recovery stories with you.

We would like to highlight the support and encouragement of our own families who have taught us first-hand how valuable family support can be; the collaboration of the staff of the FED; and the commitment of the Schizophrenia Program at CAMH for believing that families matter and for supporting our efforts to provide family-centred care. Particular thanks to April Collins, Thomas Hall, Marilyn Dakers-Hayward, Kate Kitchen, Helen McGee, Terry-Lee Marttinen, Dr. George Papatheodorou and Janine Robb for helping us bring this to completion. Some of the information has been adapted from the work of the Early Psychosis Prevention and Intervention

Centre (EPPIC) in Melbourne whose staff members have been pioneers in this area.

In particular, we would like to acknowledge Dr. Patrick McGorry. We would also like to acknowledge the Schizophrenia Society of Ontario's contributions.

Many thanks to Caroline Hebblethwaite, who managed the development and production of this manual from its inception. Her ongoing encouragement and skill are much appreciated. And last but never least, our appreciation to our editor Jacquelyn Waller-Vintar and our art director and designer Mara Korkola.

*Sabrina Baker*
*Lisa Martens*

# Introduction

As a starting point, it is important to talk about what we mean by "family."

When we use the term "family," we mean whoever the ill person says is part of his or her family, based on a strong, enduring connection with that person. This broad definition may include people who are not biologically related to one another.

## WHAT IS PSYCHOSIS?

The word "psychosis" is used to describe conditions that affect the mind when there has been some loss of contact—a break—with reality. Psychosis can lead to confused thinking, false beliefs, hallucinations, changes in feelings and changed behaviour. About three out of every 100 people will experience a psychotic episode in their lifetime. Psychosis can happen to anyone. It is important to remember that psychosis can be treated.

## WHAT IS FIRST EPISODE PSYCHOSIS?

First episode psychosis refers to the first time someone experiences psychotic symptoms or has a psychotic episode. A person experiencing a first episode of psychosis may not understand what is happening to him or her, and may feel confused and distressed. Mental and emotional problems are often like physical problems: the sooner they are treated, the better the chance of recovery. The longer psychosis is left untreated, the more the person's life is disrupted. Delays in treatment may lead to a slower and less complete recovery.

# PHASES OF A PSYCHOTIC ILLNESS

A psychotic episode occurs in three phases. The length of each phase varies from person to person.

*Phase 1, the prodomal phase,* occurs before psychotic symptoms appear. There are vague signs that "things are not quite right" and individuals may have a range of mild or infrequent symptoms. Many family members say it is easier to identify this phase when you look back on your loved one's behaviour. When it is happening, it is often hard for family members and professionals to see the difference between normal teenage behaviour and the early warning signs that come before a first break.

*Phase 2, the acute phase,* is when the person has clear psychotic symptoms such as hallucinations, delusions or confused thinking. He or she often has trouble with day-to-day activities. This is usually the time that your relative comes for treatment.

*Phase 3* is the recovery phase. Recovery is a gradual process, which varies from person to person. While symptoms are treatable, recovery does not always mean "cure" or a total disappearance of symptoms. Some people who have a psychotic episode will never have another one. For other people, psychosis will be a long-term, manageable condition.

# WHAT IS RECOVERY?

Recovery is a gradual process that is unique for each person. Recovery refers to the goal of helping your relative reintegrate into the community, and getting back to a meaningful and fulfilling life. It also means ensuring that you and the rest of your family continue to thrive and return to your usual activities. There may be many setbacks during this time. Family members who have been through their loved one's recovery say it can resemble a roller-coaster ride.

A parent writes:

> *I want my son to be better, of course, and I grasp at any indication that he is making progress, which sometimes seems so little and so slow. I have come to realize that this is not going to be a straight path*

*and that there will be ups and downs for him and therefore for me too. I had lost a big part of him for a while and it could happen again, but for now I see more of him returning, and more and more good days than bad, which wasn't the case not so many months ago. I remember when I heard him singing one day, and I knew that things were changing. He was able to hold some work for a short time again recently, which was a good milestone too, and the momentum is building. Someone recently said that none of us would be the same people we were before the first episode. I suppose time and elusive patience will reveal just what that means.*

Although you can help your relative, you cannot make someone well. Your relative has to be active in his or her own recovery.

# Families: partners in care

It is important to know that **families do not cause psychosis**. However, studies have shown that adopting a psychoeducational approach—incorporating psychotherapy, education about the illness and recovery, and supporting your relative's recovery—will improve outcomes for your relative and improve the family's well-being. Families can be an invaluable part of the treatment team. Psychosis affects every family member and how they relate to other family members. We know that when family members work together and work with their loved one's treatment team, they not only help in the recovery process but can help make a more positive outcome for their loved one.

## THE FIRST EPISODE PSYCHOSIS FAMILY PROGRAM

Most first episode and early intervention programs have family programs as part of their discharge planning for mental health clients. Since most people who have had a first episode of psychosis are young and still living at or near their family home, they are often happy for their family to be involved in their treatment. However, sometimes the person chooses not to have their family involved in their care. That does not stop family members from caring about them and giving feedback to the treatment team. Families can still receive education, support and counselling in their own right from a family worker without breaching their relative's confidentiality.

The goals of family programs are to:

· help the family as a whole to cope by providing education, support and/or counselling on an as-needed basis
· help family members to become partners in their relative's recovery process
· minimize disruption to family life
· lessen the risk of long-term grief and stress.

Each family is different: a family program should respect and pay attention to these differences, while giving you the support you need and deserve. It should build on the strengths, resilience and relationships within your family. Most of all, a good family program will recognize that you have special knowledge of your loved one, and include you in the recovery plan.

# PART I

# Promoting recovery for your relative with psychosis

# Promoting recovery

Treatment for young people who have experienced psychosis is designed for each particular person, at her or his age, at her or his stage of the illness. It brings in as many aspects of life as possible. This means that all the determinants of mental health are taken into consideration. These include:

- biological
- social
- psychological
- recreational
- economic
- vocational
- spiritual
- intellectual.

Your observations, input and recommendations on all aspects of treatment and in all phases of the illness are vital. Treatment team members recognize that, in most cases, you know your relatives best and will likely be the ones to support the ill relative throughout treatment and recovery.

## Medication

Medication is a major part of treatment. Since psychosis has a strong biological component, *antipsychotic medications* are the cornerstone of treatment. In general, they are safe to use, but as with all medications, they have risks as well as benefits. We encourage you to discuss with the physician the specific benefits and risks of the medication being prescribed. Printed material is also available for you to read.

## TYPES OF MEDICATION

Today, the treatment for a first episode of psychosis usually involves the use of newer antipsychotic medications (called *atypical antipsychotics*). The most commonly used atypical antipsychotics are olanzapine, risperidone, and quetiapine. Paliperidone and ziprasidone and aripiprazole have recently been made available in Canada, although private health insurance coverage for them is limited. The older *typical antipsychotics* are still used, especially when patients do not respond to the atypical medications or experience too many side-effects to them. Clozapine is another medication that is only used when two or more other antipsychotic medications are not effective. Its use is closely watched because it often has a dangerous side-effect. Antipsychotic medications come in tablet, liquid or injectable form.

## HOW LONG WILL IT TAKE FOR THE MEDICATION TO WORK?

The goal of medication treatment of psychosis is to improve symptoms. A positive response to antipsychotics may occur after a few weeks; however, it may be many weeks before the full effect of the medication is seen. Much of the improvement will occur in the first six months of treatment. The physician needs to closely monitor the medication as it takes effect. Some people may respond positively to the first medication prescribed, while others may need a change in medication if they do not respond. Your observations of your ill relative will be invaluable at this point in recovery.

## SIDE-EFFECTS

The best medication treatment plan starts with the lowest possible dose of antipsychotic medication and then slowly increases the dose if necessary. The goal is to relieve symptoms as much as possible while keeping side-effects to a minimum. Some side-effects may still occur. Most of them are not serious and will go away as your relative continues the medication.

Serious side-effects to watch for and talk to your relative's doctor about (the doctor and treatment team members will also be looking for these signs) are:
- weight gain
- changes in glucose metabolism / increased risk for diabetes
- changes in cholesterol
- spasms in the eye or neck muscles, which can also affect swallowing and breathing—known as acute dystonic reactions
- muscle spasms, severe rigidity or shaking—known as extrapyramidal side-effects (EPS)
- restlessness—known as akathesia
- bizarre facial, tongue and hand movements—known as tardive dyskinesia.

Common side-effects of antipsychotic medications include:
- drowsiness or lethargy
- dizziness
- dry mouth
- blurred vision
- constipation
- nausea or heartburn
- hormone changes
- changes in sexual desire and sexual performance.

Other less common side-effects that require immediate medical attention include:
- skin rash or itching
- unusual headache, persistent dizziness or fainting
- vomiting, loss of appetite, lethargy, weakness, fever or flu-like symptoms
- soreness of the mouth, gums or throat
- yellow tinge in the eyes or to the skin
- dark-coloured urine
- inability to pass urine (for more than 24 hours)
- inability to have a bowel movement (for more than two to three days)
- fever (high temperature) with muscle stiffness/rigidity.

## What will happen if side-effects occur?

If your relative finds the side-effects are too much for her or him to handle, it's important to talk to the treatment team. In some cases, the physician may lower the dose, or prescribe medications to reduce the side-effects or even switch to another medication. Your relative will be closely checked, whether in hospital or as an outpatient, to make sure the medication is working and that side-effects are kept to a minimum.

# STOPPING MEDICATION

## What happens if your relative stops taking medication?

Medications do not cure psychosis. They control symptoms as long as the person keeps taking the medication. If your relative stops taking the medication, the symptoms will either become worse or, if symptoms have gone away, they will come back. For some people, the symptoms return immediately, while for others it can take days or weeks for them to come back. When symptoms come back, it's called a relapse. The key way to prevent a relapse is for the person to take medication as prescribed. (See tips for preventing relapse on page 16.)

## Why do people stop taking their medication?

One tricky part of caring for a loved one after a first episode of psychosis is getting her or him to take the antipsychotic medication prescribed by the doctor. She or he may need encouragement to take the antipsychotics. Some of the reasons why young people have difficulty taking medication and taking it regularly include:

· not believing that they have an illness
· not understanding the medication will help
· feeling so well after taking medication that they think that they no longer need it
· stigma
· the cost of the medication (if a drug plan is not available)
· fear of loss of control
· resentment about having to take medication
· symptoms of the illness (e.g., believing medications are poisonous)
· unpleasant side-effects
· problems with memory, concentration and focus due to the illness.

TIPS: What you can do to assist loved ones in taking medications

There are a number of things that you can do to help your loved one in taking medications. You can, for instance:

· encourage taking the medications regularly, without nagging
· help set up memory aids for taking medications (e.g., suggest that he or she use a pill box organizer, put medications by his or her toothbrush, or set an alarm on a watch)
· suggest taking medication at the same time each day
· anticipate that at some point your relative may not want to take medication
· keep the lines of communication open
· give reminders of the positives of taking the medication and the risks of not taking the medication
· talk with the treatment team when concerns come up and tell your relative to do the same
· get all the information you can about the medication—from the doctor, treatment team, your pharmacist, even the Internet—and go over the benefits, risks and side-effects (don't be afraid to ask for this information, or to ask questions based on what you have read from other sources)
· know that it is usually hard for people to accept that they have an illness and need to take medication on a daily basis
· try to be patient and encourage your relative to talk about his or her feelings about the medication to the treatment team
· speak to your relative and the treatment team about the pros and cons of quick-dissolving formulations and injectable medications.

# INTERACTION WITH OTHER MEDICATIONS

Other medications can increase side-effects of the antipsychotics and may also alter the effect of the antipsychotic. Tell the family doctor, the pharmacist or the dentist that your relative is taking antipsychotic medication. People taking antipsychotics should always check with the psychiatrist or pharmacist before taking any other drugs, including over-the-counter medications such as cold remedies.

# Street drugs and alcohol

Many young people, including those with psychosis, use alcohol and street drugs. Alcohol and other drugs do not interact well with prescribed medication. Some drugs such as cocaine and ecstasy have more serious physical side-effects, such as heart problems. Using alcohol and street drugs can harm your relative's physical health, cost a lot of money and ruin social networks. Intravenous drug use has the added danger of exposing people to many illnesses including hepatitis and HIV (the virus that causes AIDS). The most commonly abused street drug is marijuana. For most people, occasionally using marijuana doesn't affect health or functioning. However, for people with a psychotic illness, marijuana even in small doses can make recovery more difficult. Using marijuana may increase the risk of a psychotic episode.

Despite all these bad effects, many young people with psychosis continue to use alcohol and other drugs. Many ill people don't do it for fun or to fit in, they do it as a way to *self-medicate*. For example, some may use marijuana to decrease the anxiety of living with voices. They may still have the urge to self-medicate even after the best treatment plan has been found, since they may still have some symptoms.

## CO-OCCURRING SUBSTANCE USE AND MENTAL HEALTH PROBLEMS

Young people getting treatment for psychosis may need professional help for their substance use problems. When people have co-occurring substance use and mental health problems (in Canada, this is called concurrent disorders), quitting alcohol or other drug use is usually the best long-term goal. However, many young people may not be motivated to decrease or stop their substance use, so clinicians may—at least in the short term—use a *harm reduction* approach. This involves reducing the harmful effects of alcohol or other drug use without expecting someone to give up the substance completely.

The ill person will need treatment for both the substance use and mental health problems at the same time. He or she will also need patience and support from family and friends. Services are available to help families cope with a substance use problem and its impact on the whole family.

If your relative has a substance use problem:
· talk openly about the use of alcohol and street drugs with your relative and the treatment team
· encourage your relative to get information about the effects of alcohol and other drugs on his or her mental and physical health
· discuss the option of substance use treatment with your relative and the treatment team
· encourage your relative to attend one of the many self-help groups that are available to deal with substance use issues; some are abstinence-based (e.g., Alcoholics Anonymous) while others have a harm reduction approach
· encourage social and recreational activities that do not centre on alcohol or other drug use
· do not offer alcohol or other drugs, regardless of how harmless you believe them to be; drugs such as marijuana can trigger a relapse in a person recovering from a psychotic episode and further complicate recovery.

A family member writes:

> From our experience, we are aware that both drug and mental rehabilitation are precarious, unpredictable processes. Taking a "tough love" approach in dealing with our son was one of the hardest decisions we have ever had to make in our lives. We refused to take our son home until he was willing to enrol in a drug rehabilitation program. At the time, he switched from shelter to shelter and occasionally slept on the street.

> He agreed to the conditions that we set for him in order to return home. He agreed to take his antipsychotic medication every day, continue to remain sober by attending his drug rehabilitation program and participate in the GED [Graduate Equivalency Diploma] program. He knew that we were serious about him adhering to these conditions. The combination of all these activities worked wonders for him. His determination to "get back on track" was strong and we were committed to help him in his recovery as much as we could. As parents, we need the strength to handle the misfortune of having two sons succumb to the lure of the drug culture and to have both suffer from mental illness.

# Psychosocial rehabilitation

Along with medication, people who have had an episode of psychosis need help to get back to day-to-day living. It's important for your loved one to learn to be independent again. Getting back to independent day-to-day life requires help in many areas. Psychosocial rehabilitation is the term for help that focuses on areas of your relative's life that are not biological. Your relative may need help that is psychological, vocational, relational, spiritual, social, environmental or recreational—all of which are explained in this section.

The type of services your relative accesses—and when she or he chooses to access them—will depend largely on what she or he is looking for and where he or she is in the stages of recovery. Services in some outpatient programs include counselling, lifeskills training, help with returning to school or work, recreation and social planning, and help with finding and using government services and community resources.

Education and support for families is also a vital part of psychosocial rehabilitation. In some cases, psychosocial services are available to families, as well as clients.

Family members may want their relative to use these services before he or she is ready to join them. Families may struggle with trying to respect their relative's right to refuse services and make that choice independently, and their own desire to see their relative get back to his or her normal functioning.

## CASE MANAGEMENT

Many early psychosis or mental health programs use a clinical case management model for delivering and co-ordinating services for your relative. The case manager assesses your relative's needs on an ongoing basis and provides and/or co-ordinates the services your relative needs.

## SUPPORTIVE COUNSELLING

Supportive counselling is used to help people learn about psychosis, its treatment, and how to cope with symptoms. Supportive counselling is focused on the present, not on what happened in early childhood or complicated psychological issues. The focus of the work is on helping the person cope with his or her psychosis and set short-term goals. Art, pet and music therapy can be used to allow creative expression, which is important for recovery. Supportive counseling can be done both individually and in a group format.

## SOCIAL SKILLS TRAINING

You may have noticed that your loved one has regressed to an earlier developmental stage. Many young people with a psychotic illness need help in developing life and social skills. Young people who have difficulty being with other people may need social skills training to get used to relating to others in social settings. Others who are learning to live on their own may find that life skills training (e.g., managing their finances or learning to cook) will help them to become independent again.

## EDUCATION

Many young people are still enrolled in high school, college or university when they have a first episode and need help to re-enter the school system. Your relative may need support from the treatment team and the family to decide when to return to class, how many classes to take, and what kinds of additional supports and accommodations (changes at school that would help your relative such as a more flexible timetable, more frequent breaks from the classroom, use of a tape recorder) are needed. High schools, colleges and universities often require some communication with a treatment team member to set this up. The inpatient social worker at the hospital or your relative's case manager can also help to locate alternative schools, enrol your relative in a college or university and connect with other educational services.

You may need to consider changing your expectations for your relative's future. As he or she recovers, there is no way to know if a relapse is in the future. Sometimes this illness creates a need for low-stress situations that can also apply to future employment. Work closely with your relative and the treatment team to set up realistic goals and expectations.

# CAREER AND EMPLOYMENT SUPPORT

Vocational (career) counselling and rehabilitation are needed to promote recovery and get your relative back in the swing of community life. Young people are often looking for or in the middle of choosing a career when psychosis strikes. For a person with a psychotic illness, this rite of passage can be seriously disrupted.

Your case manager, the treatment team and other people in the community can help your relative through this challenging time with:

· support and counselling around his or her career interests
· help getting ready for re-entry into the workforce
· help with finding and keeping a job
· referrals to sheltered employment, youth employment services and volunteer placements.

Finding out what kind of career and job help your relative wants usually means meeting with the treatment team and a supportive employment specialist and/or occupational therapist. They can explore your relative's own interests and readiness for work.

# RECREATION THERAPY

Psychosis affects every aspect of life. Part of recovery is your relative getting back to his or her social circle and creating new ways to get involved in enjoyable activities again. Recreation therapy is an important part of all phases of treatment. Recreation therapists provide one-on-one counselling, assessment and group opportunities. Examples of activities include art therapy, sports and camping.

# HOUSING AND SOCIAL SERVICES

Practical issues such as the need to find housing or get financial help add to the stress of a mental illness. A social worker or case manager can provide information and make referrals for your relative. There are many different housing options—private rooms or apartments, boarding homes, co-ops and group homes. Your relative may need help in applying for subsidized or supportive housing, social assistance, employment insurance, disability benefits or student loans.

# STAYING WELL

For people recovering from a psychotic episode, staying well and preventing a relapse is most important. A relapse is when psychotic symptoms come back or get worse. The most common reason for a relapse is not taking medication. Other triggers include the use of alcohol and/or street drugs, stress and loss of support. The chance of a relapse is highest in the first year of recovery. You and your relative can get extra support and counselling on how to stay well and lessen the chance of future relapses.

# EARLY WARNING SIGNS OF A RELAPSE

A relapse into psychosis rarely happens without warning. Get to know your relative's behaviour patterns and learn about the symptoms of the illness so you and your family can identify early warning signs of psychosis. Learning about the signs and getting quick attention can reduce the chance of a full-blown relapse and may prevent a hospital admission. See Appendix 3 for a form that will help you keep track of these signs.

You and your relative should talk with the treatment team about early warning signs and symptoms of relapse. Sometimes there are few outward signs; only the ill person knows the inner symptoms. These inner symptoms could be voices or sounds your relative hears, or things he or she sees or feels that no one else does. These symptoms are apparent to the ill person only, and they are often unique to each person. You should encourage your relative to recognize his or her warning symptoms and tell the family and the team what they are.

Common early warning signs include:
· feeling more tense, nervous or irritable than usual
· feeling less able to concentrate or pay attention
· needing more time alone, and withdrawing from people he or she usually feels comfortable around
· increased sensitivity to light or sounds
· poor sleep (more sleep or less sleep than usual), which is often accompanied by vivid, frightening nightmares
· increased psychotic symptoms (e.g., the unusual thoughts or experiences caused by the illness happen more often or become more intense: the person can't easily get them out of her or his head).

Adapted with permission from G. Remington and A. Collins, *Learning about Schizophrenia*, 1999.

TIPS: Staying well strategies for preventing relapse

Your family and your relative who is recovering from first episode psychosis can use a number of strategies to avoid a relapse. These include:

- taking medications as prescribed
- attending psychosocial rehabilitation programs that help with treatment and recovery
- not taking street drugs and alcohol
- maintaining good physical health and self-care (e.g., eating properly, getting enough sleep)
- establishing a routine
- reducing stress as much as possible
- developing good communication and problem-solving skills to deal with stress
- having someone to talk to
- developing social support
- having good information sources
- having a stable place to live
- preserving a sense of hope
- having a meaningful occupation, study, work or hobby.

# SOME COMMON DIFFICULTIES IN RECOVERY

People in recovery often experience:

- impatience (recovery takes time)
- depression and isolation
- social anxiety (feeling uneasy when with people)
- lowered self-esteem
- lack of insight into their illness
- non-acceptance of their illness
- a lack of desire to work with the treatment team.

# Crisis intervention

A crisis is when the symptoms get much worse and cause distress and disruption in the home. Your loved one can make threats of suicide or violence toward others. It is a frightening experience for both the ill person and the family. If this happens, get medical attention immediately.

There are some things that you can do to help the ill person and calm the situation before the person harms herself or himself, or is aggressive toward

## TIPS: Dealing with a crisis

Things to remember when dealing with a crisis:
- Try to remain calm.
- Give space by not hovering over the person or getting too close.
- Ask others to leave the room and shut off the TV and radio to reduce distractions.
- Speak slowly and clearly, using simple sentences.
- Invite the person to sit down and talk about what is bothering him or her.
  Things not to do:
- Don't shout, patronize, criticize or insult the person.
- Don't block the doorway (you should allow an escape route).
- Don't make too much eye contact.
- Don't be too emotional.

Adapted with permission from the Schizophrenia Society of Canada (2003), *Learning about Schizophrenia: Rays of Hope. A Reference Manual for Families and Caregivers*, 3rd Revised Edition. Markham, Ontario: Author.

others or damages property. The following suggestions will help you to cope if your relative is becoming agitated and distressed. If the safety of the individual or others is at risk, disengage and seek help.

# Self-harm and aggression

## SUICIDE

A common fear for many families is the issue of suicide. There are different reasons why a person experiencing a first episode of psychosis or a relapse thinks about ending his or her life. The person may be desperately unhappy about the illness and its impact on his or her life; the person may be responding to psychotic symptoms (e.g., voices telling the person to harm himself or herself); or the person may unintentionally kill himself or herself while crying out for help. Some suicides are planned, while others are done on impulse. All talks of suicide or self-harm must be taken seriously.

Warning signs:
· feelings of depression, worthlessness or hopelessness about the future
· getting affairs in order
· giving away treasured possessions
· talking about hearing voices that tell the person to do dangerous things to himself or herself
· talking about having special powers (e.g., the ability to fly)
· talking about suicide or what death would be like
· having a previous history of suicidal behaviour.

### How to help

Talk openly about suicide with your relative and the treatment team. An honest discussion about suicide doesn't encourage the person to think about suicide or act on suicidal thoughts. In fact, it encourages him or her to open up about suicidal impulses. Talking about suicide also provides everyone with direction and support about what to do.

If you discover your relative after a suicide attempt:
· call 911
· perform CPR, if you know how.

After you have dealt with the emergency:
- get support for yourself; don't try to handle it on your own
- contact the treatment team
- consider joining or reconnecting with a support group.

## VIOLENCE

Threats of violence are the exception rather than the norm. Most people are passive, anxious and withdrawn when they are having a psychotic episode. The best predictor of violence is whether or not a person has a history of violence. If there is a history of violence, find out:
- what the circumstances or triggers were
- whether alcohol or other drugs were involved
- if the person was taking medication.

The answers to these questions will help in predicting future (if any) violent behaviour and developing a crisis intervention plan.

There are times when aggression may occur. The person may be responding to psychotic symptoms (e.g., a paranoid delusion in which the person truly feels others are trying to harm him or her). Sometimes, the aggression may have nothing to do with symptoms but is an expression of anger or an attempt to control others in order to get what he or she wants. Regardless of the reason, the first priority is to protect all family members, including your relative. This may mean leaving the room or the house and calling the police. If it is not safe to take the person to the hospital, calling the police may be the only option.

# Strategies for dealing with emergencies

## CRISIS INTERVENTION PLANNING

Knowing what to do in case of an emergency—before it actually happens—can be very helpful for everyone, especially the person with psychosis. If you talk to your relative, your family and the treatment team about a crisis plan, you can reduce the level of distress for everyone. Discuss who to call, where to go and the names and numbers of emergency contacts (e.g., police, psychiatrist, support worker, other family or friends) who can be of support. Make plans for the care of other family members (e.g., children, elderly parents). Some families find it extremely helpful to keep a list of important phone numbers (e.g., friends, health care workers, police) on a small card or piece of paper, and put it in their own wallet, and/or their relative's wallet, in case of an emergency. For a sample crisis card, see Appendix 4.

### A NOTE ABOUT MENTAL HEALTH LEGISLATION

In Canada, each province has its own mental health legislation, so the rules vary from province to province. In this guide we talk about how mental health laws work in Ontario. If you live outside Ontario, provincial offices of the Canadian Mental Health Association (CMHA) and websites of provincial ministries of health are sources of information. Here are some useful links:

· **Alberta**
*The Mental Health Act of Alberta: A Guide for Consumers and Caregivers* (available online through CMHA Alberta)
· **British Columbia**
*BC's Mental Health Act in Plain Language* (available online through CMHA BC)
· **Manitoba**
www.gov.mb.ca/health/mh/act.html
· **New Brunswick**
www.ahsc.health.nb.ca/Programs/MentalHealth/rights.shtml
· **Newfoundland and Labrador**
www.health.gov.nl.ca/health/mhcta
· **Nova Scotia**
www.gov.ns.ca/health/mhs/ipta.asp
· **Prince Edward Island**
*Islanders Guide to the Mental Health Act*
www.gov.pe.ca/publications/getpublication.php3?number=118
· **Quebec**
*Mental Illness: A Regional Handbook for Families* (available from CMHA Quebec)
· **Saskatchewan**
www.health.gov.sk.ca/rr_your_prsnl_rights_mhsa.html

## Ontario mental health laws

There are three main acts that outline rights with respect to mental health services:

- The **Mental Health Act** is a set of rules that gives doctors and psychiatric facilities certain powers and gives patients particular rights. These laws apply to general hospital psychiatric units and psychiatric hospitals but not to mental health clinics. The Mental Health Act deals with many inpatient issues, including:
  - when someone can be taken and admitted to a psychiatric facility involuntarily
  - how someone can be kept in the hospital
  - who can see a patient's records in the facility, and how to arrange to see the records
  - a patient's right to information and right to appeal being involuntarily admitted, held in a facility, denied access to records and so on.
- The **Health Care Consent Act** deals with rules for consenting, or agreeing, to treatment.
- The **Substitute Decisions Act** deals with how decisions can be made for someone and the appointment of powers of attorney for personal care and property.

From Centre for Addiction and Mental Health (2003). *Challenges and Choices: Finding Mental Health Services in Ontario.*

# INVOLVING THE POLICE

The best solution when there is a crisis is to get your relative to agree to see the doctor or go to the emergency department. If your loved one refuses to go to the hospital, and if you believe that there is a safety risk, call the police.

Many of you who have had to make the decision to call the police have reported how uncomfortable this has made you feel. However, given the risk of injury to your ill relative and to others, most people agree that it was the only option.

The police might not take your relative to the hospital if he or she is not in an acutely psychotic or distressed state when the police arrive. If the police do not take your relative to hospital, you can go to a Justice of the Peace at the nearest courthouse and request that an Order for Examination (Form 2) be filled out. Based on the information provided by you or other witnesses,

## TIPS: Calling the police

· Let your relative know you are calling the police. This may calm him or her down.
· Explain to the police the need for emergency medical attention and tell them that your relative has a mental illness.
· Give a brief description of events (e.g., threatening to hurt self or others).
· State the need for help to get the person to the hospital.
· Tell the police if your relative is armed.
· Be prepared for handcuffs.
· Be aware that an assessment does not necessarily lead to a hospital admission, and that your relative could be charged.
· Try to get to the hospital emergency room and speak directly to the doctor or emergency staff.
· The police must stay with the ill person in the emergency room until an assessment is carried out. They must report all facts to the hospital staff.

Adapted with permission from the Schizophrenia Society of Canada (2003). *Learning about Schizophrenia: Rays of Hope. A Reference Manual for Families and Caregivers*, 3rd Revised Edition. Markham, Ontario: Author.

the Justice of the Peace decides whether your ill relative meets the legal definition of a danger to self or others or of being unable to care for himself or herself. If so, a Form 2 is completed, giving the police the mandate to bring the person to the hospital for an assessment. It is helpful if you can accompany your relative to the hospital.

Even if the police bring your relative to the hospital for an assessment, he or she might not be admitted. If this happens, it is usually because the ill person does not meet the criteria for involuntary committal and does not want to be admitted as a voluntary patient. For more information about committal to hospital, see page 23.

You may find yourself in a position where your relative is in trouble with the law. You may feel overwhelmed and unprepared to deal with this situation. Other family members may feel embarrassed or ashamed and may not know how to advocate for help for your relative. Remember to speak to your relative's treatment team about your concerns. Often when problems such as this arise, it is because your loved one has not been taking his or her medication.

For more about what to do if your relative comes into contact with the law, see *The Forensic Mental Health System in Ontario: An Information Guide* (www.camh.net/Care_Treatment/Resources_clients_families_friends/Forensic _Mental_Health_Ontario/index.html).

# Hospitalization

In a perfect world young people who are experiencing their first episode of psychosis are cared for in the familiarity of their own homes. Fortunately, this is often possible with the support of psychiatric and community services. However, sometimes treatment at home is not appropriate, especially if there are concerns about safety. When the young person's own safety or the safety of others is at risk, hospitalization is the only alternative. The purpose of hospitalization is to ensure safety, to stabilize the person and to start the recovery process as quickly as possible. The recovery process continues in the community after discharge.

## CAN YOUR RELATIVE BE MADE TO STAY IN HOSPITAL AGAINST HIS OR HER WILL?

A person can be admitted to hospital as an involuntary, or certified, patient if he or she is seen to be a danger to himself or herself or others, or is so impaired in his or her ability to maintain self-care (e.g., not eating) that physical harm is likely to occur because of the mental health problem. This means that the person is made to stay in hospital against his or her will as long as the person continues to meet one of more of these criteria. All involuntary clients are visited by a rights advisor who informs them of their rights. Clients have the legal right to challenge their involuntary status and bring their case to a Consent and Capacity Board hearing, which will either uphold the involuntary status or revoke it. If it is upheld, the client remains in hospital. If it is revoked, the client can either leave hospital or remain as a voluntary client.

A person who **does not** meet the criteria for involuntary committal has two options:
· The person can agree to stay in hospital as a voluntary patient and receive treatment.

- The person can leave. This may mean signing out of hospital "against medical advice" (AMA).

    Anyone who is not an involuntary client has the right to refuse treatment and leave the hospital.

    You can find more information about the law and mental health in Ontario on the Internet:

- Consent and Capacity Board: www.ccboard.on.ca/scripts/english/index.asp
- Psychiatric Patient Advocate Office: www.ppao.gov.on.ca/en-index.html
- *Challenges and Choices: Finding Mental Health Services in Ontario* has a section on understanding client rights under Ontario law (www.camh.net/ Care_Treatment/Resources_clients_families_friends/Challenges_and_Choice s/challenges_choices_rights.html) and a summary of common legal forms (www.camh.net/Care_Treatment/Resources_clients_families_friends/ Challenges_and_Choices/challenges_choices_appclegalform.html).

# WHAT TO EXPECT DURING YOUR RELATIVE'S HOSPITALIZATION

Being admitted to hospital and treatment can be confusing and frightening for you and your relative. When your loved one is admitted to an inpatient unit, he or she is assigned a primary nurse, a psychiatrist and a social worker. Personal valuables, money and potentially harmful items (e.g., knives, belts) are locked up and returned when the client is discharged. It is suggested that you take your relative's valuables—with the exception of a small amount of spending money—home with you. Your relative will be given a tour of the unit and a description of the ward practices, services and programs. You can also request a tour of the facility and are encouraged to speak with staff regarding unit practices, programs and services.

   Your relative is given a thorough medical exam, including a physical checkup, blood and urine tests, and possibly CT and MRI scans, to ensure that psychotic symptoms are not the result of some other illness or substance use. Throughout the course of hospitalization, your relative will be interviewed and assessed by the treatment team. The interviews help the treatment team:

- arrive at a diagnosis
- determine the appropriate course of treatment
- decide whether your relative has the ability to make treatment decisions

· determine whether further hospitalization is necessary.

Programs on the inpatient unit are tailored to the needs of each person. The inpatient unit staff:

· identifies and treats symptoms of psychosis
· educates you and your ill relative about the illness
· supports and promotes recovery
· provides one-to-one support or counselling
· provides a range of groups and activities
· connects you and your relative to outpatient services, such as case management and psychiatric follow-up.

## Confidentiality

The treatment team may ask to interview family members, or the family can request to meet with the treatment team. However, your relative has the right to decide what, if any, information is shared with his or her family and friends. If your relative refuses to let staff speak with you, the staff should continue to talk to your relative about allowing communication with you. If your relative still refuses to allow staff to speak with you, you and other family members can receive education about psychosis and can still benefit from support and counselling to help you to cope with the illness.

There are situations where restrictions on release of information can be lifted. If your relative is found to be incapable to consent to his or her own treatment, then a substitute decision-maker (SDM) can make decisions on behalf of the person. In this situation, the family member who is the SDM can communicate with the team about treatment issues without the relative's permission. Your relative's consent to release information to other family members who do not fulfil the SDM role is still required. The Psychiatric Patient Advocate Office website (www.ppao.gov.on.ca/inf-sub.html) has information about what is involved in becoming an SDM.

Note that, even though a team may not be allowed to give information to family members, a treatment team member can collect information from anyone regarding a person who is at risk of harming himself, herself or others, or is at risk of causing impairment to himself or herself. The team member may not be in a position to discuss specific details about the patient with you, but would be obliged to share the information and the source with the patient.

# DISCHARGE PLANNING

Plans for discharge from hospital will be discussed with your loved one, the family and the treatment team as soon as possible. Discharge planning includes such issues as:

· where your relative will live after hospitalization
· referrals to outpatient support services
· how to manage at home
· medication
· financial support
· the young person's goals (e.g., school)
· support services available for family
· developing a crisis plan should difficulties arise.

## Follow-up services

A good follow-up outpatient program will include assigning a psychiatrist and case manager as well as providing psychosocial rehabilitation. These services are designed to assist your relative with recovery and to provide support, education and/or counselling to your family. The services beyond those of a psychiatrist and a case manager vary widely depending on where you live. Any questions related to discharge can be directed to the unit social worker.

## Respecting diversity

Many clients and their families require culturally appropriate care and information. These could include:

· language interpreters
· religious services in multiple faiths
· special dietary needs (e.g., ethnic/religious, vegetarian, diabetic)
· written literature in preferred language (where available)
· referral to appropriate outpatient supports in keeping with cultural, gender, sexual orientation and disability needs.

Family members should discuss their own and their relative's special needs with the treatment team.

# How to work with mental health professionals

The goal of the treatment team is to establish a partnership with you and your relative in order to best meet everyone's needs. While in hospital, your relative is assigned a psychiatrist, a primary nurse and a social worker. If your loved one is an outpatient, he or she will be assigned a psychiatrist and a case manager. Write down their names and contact information. For inpatients, the families' primary contact is the unit social worker. For outpatients, the families' primary contact is the case manager.

## Treatment team members

In a team-based model, the team members meet regularly to review your relative's progress. The psychiatrist is a member of the team with overall responsibility for medications. The primary nurse or case manager co-ordinates care for the person with psychosis. The unit social worker (and a family worker, if available) does more intensive family work with individuals and groups. Treatment teams include some, or all, of the following types of mental health professionals:

**Case manager:** works with outpatient clients to provide psychiatric care along with the client's psychiatrist. A case manager can be a nurse, social worker or occupational therapist. Case managers work with the client to co-ordinate a comprehensive rehabilitation program. Case managers may also talk with the family.

**Chaplain:** provides spiritual and religious care to clients of all faiths. Services include individual and group support, and worship services for clients and families.

**Dietitian:** works with the treatment team to assess, consult, treat and advocate for clients and families. The dietitian works with clients and families to improve health and quality of life (e.g., assessing clients at nutritional risk, prescribing therapeutic diets, teaching nutritional health, treating and monitoring nutritionally related conditions, advocating for healthy inpatient menus and a variety of community supports).

**Employment specialist:** works one-on-one with clients toward employment goals by providing intake, vocational counselling, job searches, job development, employment support and coaching. The employment specialist (ES) also plans and prepares employment-related workshops for clients. The ES works with other agencies, vocational staff and interdisciplinary teams.

**Family worker:** provides support, education and counselling to individuals, couples and families. Family counselling is provided on an individual basis as well as in a group format to help the family become an ally in their loved one's recovery and gain support for themselves to promote their own recovery. Family workers, many of whom are social workers, have expertise in family systems work and are able to work with families with more complex issues (e.g., family members may also have a mental illness or addictions or may have experienced trauma and other oppressions).

**Occupational therapist:** assists in the recovery process by providing assessments of functional and vocational skills, and practical strategies in returning to daily activities such as work and school.

**Peer recovery facilitator:** talks with the person who has experienced psychosis around five key peer principles: self-advocacy, education, mutual support, individual responsibility for recovery and hope. The facilitator is an individual who has personal experience or a history with mental health issues. He or she develops a non-clinical, non-hierarchical relationship with your relative based on exploring the principles surrounding recovery.

**Pharmacist:** works with the team and the central pharmacy department to provide clients with medications, and to educate them about their medications, including information on side-effects, drug interactions and how to take medications properly. In addition to counselling, the pharmacist provides physicians and other health care providers with drug information.

**Primary nurse**: works with clients, families and the treatment team to provide a comprehensive plan of care that promotes recovery. The primary nurse's role is to speak with clients and families about the ill relatives' thinking, mood and behaviour. Nursing staff work in the outpatient clinic, as part of home visiting teams and provide 24-hour care on the inpatient unit.

**Psychiatrist**: specializes in assessing, diagnosing and treating mental disorders. A psychiatrist has a medical degree and at least five years of postgraduate training in psychiatry.

**Psychologist**: provides assessment, diagnosis, interpretation of psychological tests, and therapy for people with mental illness. A psychologist engages in "talk therapy" but does not administer medications.

**Recreation therapist**: provides recreation opportunities and resources to aid in the clients' recovery and improve their health and well-being. Recreation programs can include sports and physical activities, healthy cooking, and planning and participating in inexpensive outings to local attractions and events. A major focus is placed on educating clients about appropriate recreational and leisure activities they can participate in while in the community.

**Resident**: a medical doctor receiving specialized training in psychiatry, who works closely with the multidisciplinary treatment team and is supervised by the staff psychiatrist in all aspects of care and treatment.

**Social worker**: works with clients, families and the treatment team to assess and treat clients, and assist with discharge planning issues. Social workers provide individual, group and family counselling to address issues related to treatment, recovery, relapse prevention, coping with psychosis and making connections with the community for additional resources.

**Teacher**: provides clients opportunities to earn high school credits for their secondary school diploma. Teachers provide support and accommodation for education and mental health recovery needs of clients under 21. They will know about local GED High School Equivalency Exam programs for clients ages 18 and over.

## TIPS: Working with mental health professionals

Here are some helpful hints when working with mental health professionals:

- Write things down (e.g., names, phone numbers, dates of meetings, questions).
- Ask for meetings with the team—contact the unit social worker or outpatient case manager. Bring someone who will be supportive. This will have to be permitted by your relative.
- Approach the staff if you have any concerns. If you don't get a satisfactory response, contact the unit manager or the client relations co-ordinator. Staff will provide this information.
- Offer your own observations on your relative's progress, including any side-effects he or she may be experiencing and any medical or social history that might be relevant to how he or she is coping now.
- Leave a name, contact number and brief message outlining relevant questions or concerns when contacting a treatment team member.
- Respect your relative's wishes (e.g., regarding how long or how often you visit).
- Don't criticize staff or programs in front of the ill person. Address staff directly.
- Closely monitor all young children when visiting the inpatient unit. Do not leave children and personal belongings unattended.
- Ask for specific information. If you don't understand what is being said to you, don't be embarrassed. Ask for an explanation.

# Stigma

Stigma is one of the biggest obstacles to the treatment of mental illness. The fear of being rejected and misunderstood may contribute to your relative and/or you denying that he or she has mental health problems and rejecting the treatment. Stigma is often caused by a lack of understanding of the problem and fear of the unknown. This can cause you and your relative to withdraw further and can delay the recovery process. People recovering from mental illness often have to face discrimination when trying to make friends, find work or locate goods and services in the community.

A parent writes:

> I make an effort to be as open as I can with people about S but I use my discretion. I want to be as honest as I can and educate people about the illness, but at the same time, I don't want to jeopardize S's emotional safety. For this reason, I haven't given my neighbours any details about S's illness. I find that I am less friendly and more introverted around my neighbours. I guess this is a defense mechanism— my way to cope with stigma.

Common myths surrounding mental illness include:

1. *People with mental illness are violent.* This is inaccurate since most people with a mental illness are best described as passive, withdrawn and anxious.
2. *Mental illness is a result of having a bad or immoral character.* Mental illness is biologically based and no more a product of poor character development or immorality than any other illness, such as diabetes or cancer.

3. *Bad upbringing causes mental illness.* To blame parents adds insult to injury and is inaccurate. It is not the fault of parents that young people develop mental illness, as mental illness is biologically based.

4. *People with mental illness have above or below average intelligence.* People with mental illness represent the whole spectrum of intellectual capacities.

# What can families do to deal with stigma?

TIPS: Combating stigma
· Treat the ill person as an adult. Offer love and support.
· Encourage a full range of talents and expression.
· Readjust expectations according to the person's stage of recovery.
· Learn to accept the illness. This can help your relative do the same.
· Support his or her involvement in psychoeducational and support groups.
· Attend support groups and learn as much as possible about the illness.
· Seek out supportive friends and relatives. Do not become isolated.

## EDUCATION, SUPPORT AND ADVOCACY

The key to fighting stigma at the individual, family and societal level is education and support. Young people and their families need to learn about first episode psychosis and receive emotional and practical support in order to cope with it and eventually recover.

Many mental health agencies and organizations also provide education to the public and other institutions and advocate at the political level for better treatment and services for people with mental illness and their families. Opportunities exist for people to be involved in advocacy initiatives. For more information about how you can be involved, see the resources listed under "Websites" in Appendix 2 of this guide.

# PART II

# Promoting recovery for you, the family member

# Family-focused care

## Family support

Helping your relative to recover from psychosis is a process that takes time. You may need help and support to promote your own recovery. As the saying goes, "Put your own oxygen mask on first" and then help your relative and other family members to put on their masks. This will allow you to continue to be an active participant in your relative's recovery.

Family intervention consists of two components: working with individual families and working with many families in a group. Individual family support tends to focus on the "now" and on helping families with problem-solving, coping and recovery skills. This support is usually short-term, consisting of approximately two to 12 sessions. Family therapy is helpful if your family has more complex challenges or if you have issues that existed before the onset of your relative's psychosis. This approach tends to be more long-term and is done with a professional who has expertise in family systems work. Therapy may be requested by couples, individual family members or the entire family.

Family group work includes family psychoeducational groups. These groups involve education about psychosis, treatment and recovery and provide you with emotional support. They are particularly helpful for those of you who wish to connect with other families who are going through a similar experience, since these groups are built on mutual support and sharing.

When hospitals and clinics take a family-centred approach, it means team members listen, involve and support the families' concerns, values, opinions and cultural backgrounds. All family members deserve support, education and/or counselling in their own right, even if the recovering relative chooses not to have his or her family members involved in his or her care. Family group leaders work in collaboration with you, acknowledging your strengths and expertise about your relative and your own lives.

A parent writes:

*We are invested in helping our relative return to health, but equally important is my own recovery and the need to restore joy, dignity and harmony to my life and to my family's life. Through working with the family worker, I am slowly beginning to understand the impact of my relative's mental illness on him and the rest of the family. By participating in the family group sessions, I was able to begin to share my feelings of frustration and anger, learn how vulnerable my son was to mental illness and begin to articulate my thoughts.*

*My spouse and I attend family counselling and this provides me with a process that continues to meet our needs and support us through the challenging times ahead. At each session, I am prepared to be honest, open and willing to learn and do whatever is necessary to achieve the happiness and joy I once knew. The process is difficult, but it is more difficult being alone, helpless and out of control. Having the support of the FED [First Episode Division, at CAMH] teams, one for my relative and one for me and my spouse, is critical to the recovery process. The family worker touches base with me to see how I am doing and to lend a friendly ear to hear my concerns and help me to problem-solve. I believe I am slowly making progress and I am beginning to realize that my feelings of being angry and lonely stop me from progressing in my own life. I take one day at a time and accept that progress is not perfection and that "balance" is my word for success. By actively participating in the group and individual sessions, my relationship with my husband is stronger and having someone else guide me through my emotional challenges helps me to make headway in my relative's recovery. By continuing to move forward and establish small goals, I will continue to try to find the joy, happiness, forgiveness and tolerance that I once felt and knew before these events unfolded.*

# EARLY PHASES OF ILLNESS

In the beginning, some of you may feel as if you are in a dark tunnel and worry that you may never come out into the light again. However, most families do recover from the stress involved with psychosis. Many of you have told us that it takes time for you to adjust your expectations and adapt the family structure to your relative in recovery.

## Phase 1: "Something is not quite right"

This phase occurs before psychotic symptoms develop. You may be aware that your relative is "not quite herself, that something is not quite right," as one of our family members said. You may feel anxious, worried and frightened. Families may blame their relative's difficulties on adolescence, socializing with the wrong crowd or drug use.

A parent writes:

> When S was 12 years old, he spent two months sleeping on the floor of my bedroom because he was afraid to go to bed. All of these fears seemed to resolve themselves, but I was aware that S was an anxious child, and as a mother kept an eye out for changes in his emotions. S also had difficulty paying attention—he wasn't present when you talked to him and I would often have to clap my hands, or shout his name to get his attention. He didn't seem to be aware of people's body space, often pushing me off the sidewalk when we walked together and bumping into me in the kitchen. He had difficulty making friends, and was often unhappy and felt picked on at school. Although S had his idiosyncrasies, none of them warranted professional help. He was functioning well at school, his fears ultimately resolved over time and he did have a few friends. My husband and I hoped he would eventually mature and grow out of his quirks.

## Phase 2: The appearance of psychotic symptoms

As it becomes clearer that the situation cannot be left to resolve itself, the family may start to seek help. At this stage, your relative may have clearly defined psychotic symptoms. The parent continues:

> During that summer, his behaviour became uncontrollable. He was smoking pot, it seemed to me continually—in our backyard, in the

*basement, in his bedroom. He became increasingly violent when my husband and I set down rules and regulations—punching holes in the wall, punching a hole through the glass door. There was blood everywhere. He would arrive home in the early hours of the morning, at times not coming home at all.*

*My husband and I went for counselling. We didn't know how to cope. S's behaviour was erratic and destructive to both himself and our family. We also have a younger daughter. We were afraid to kick him out of the house because he still had this childlike vulnerability. He had no street smarts. But we couldn't continue with the chaos he was causing. He started back to school (Grade 11) in September, came home with a bloody nose that he got during a fight and never returned to school. One afternoon that September, S told me that he thought that MuchMusic (a TV channel) had a camera that had the ability to watch the viewers at home. I filed this away as an interesting thought, not knowing that this was the first indication of S's decline into psychosis.*

*S's delusions and paranoid thinking increased. It became apparent to my husband and me that S needed psychiatric help. I contacted the Centre for Addiction and Mental Health in Toronto and set up an appointment for an assessment. I can remember driving S down to his first appointment. He was looking over his shoulder, convinced that people were watching him. He was extremely agitated, but convinced (as one with psychosis is) that nothing was wrong with him. S was diagnosed with first episode psychosis and prescribed risperidone. My husband and I were not sure what to think. We were deeply concerned about our son, but hoped that this was a temporary illness, caused by stress and too much pot.*

Many of you have told us that in the early phases of dealing with psychosis, you felt as though you were in "uncharted waters, feeling alone and without hope and help." It is often difficult to navigate the mental health system. You may face the stigma associated with mental illness and may pull away from your family and friends. The trauma involved in dealing with the illness can affect your family's usual coping patterns. There is an interruption of the regular individual development for your relative as well as an interruption in your family's usual development. For example, some of you may have been in the "empty nest" phase of your life, with your child or children away from home, and now find yourself with increased caregiving responsibilities. You may find yourself in a more active role when your relative is in this early stage of recovery, needing more care and support. This change in the family structure can really test its strength. It is important for you to recall how you coped with previous crises and to remind yourself of the strategies that you previously used to get through hard times. In the heat of the moment, many of you may feel disarmed and forget the resources that you already possess to help you in your time of need.

## Some common initial reactions to your relative's illness

Common initial reactions to discovering that your relative has an illness include:

- Sadness and grief: "We have lost our child. Will this illness change the hopes and dreams we have for our child and for ourselves?"
- Fear and anxiety: "How are we going to cope right now and in the future?" "Will my relative ever marry, have children and be able to work again?"
- Shame and guilt: "What have I done to cause this illness?" "I don't want to tell our family, friends, the community about our relative's illness."
- Denial: "Our relative is just lazy, not sick." "Our relative needs to pull herself together and everything will be fine again."
- Feeling overwhelmed and/or depressed: "How are we going to cope with this illness?" "I don't know what to do. It seems so hopeless."
- Remorse, blaming yourself: "Why didn't I realize that there was something wrong and seek help earlier?"
- Anger and blame: "It's his fault. He brought it on himself by hanging out with the wrong crowd and taking drugs."
- Relief: "I knew there was something wrong with my relative. Now that we know what is happening to my relative, we can begin treatment."

All these reactions are normal and appropriate. Feelings are neither right nor wrong, they just are. Remember that this is likely to be a difficult adjustment for each family member and it is important to try to treat yourself with love, understanding and compassion.

## Coping strategies

Education and support for the family is very important, particularly in the early phases of treatment. Knowledge is power. The better informed you are about your relative's illness, the better prepared you will be to navigate the treatment system and promote recovery for your relative and yourself. It is important to try to remember to separate the illness from the person.

Many of you find that you need to develop different ways of coping, and different styles of communicating with your relative to be supportive to him or her. This will likely reduce your own anxiety and help you feel more in control of yourself.

Your relative will need time to recover and probably won't be able to fully engage in all activities of daily living right away. A structured approach, which includes gradually taking on tasks and activities, usually works best. An ordered and predictable environment helps people recover from psychosis. You can get support and education on an as-needed basis to discuss these issues more fully.

## Services that may help families in the early phases of illness

Support to families during this stage optimally consists of frequent contact providing high levels of support. You will be invited to talk to a case manager, social worker or family worker about what life was like before your relative became ill. It may be a relief to tell your story in a safe environment and to describe the events leading up to your relative's first episode of psychosis. You will probably have lots of questions and worries at this time such as: What is psychosis? What causes it? What can we do to help? Will this happen again? What shall we tell other people?

Family work is tailored to meet your needs across all phases of recovery. Initial family support will likely revolve around:

· dealing with grief and loss
· adjusting to having different expectations for your relative
· reaching a shared understanding about what psychosis is
· learning about staying well
· discussing what the illness means to you
· learning how to access and negotiate the mental health system
· problem-solving on a day-to-day basis

- exploring ways of coping and managing your own stress levels
- remembering how you coped with other crises in your life
- helping your relative to become as independent and autonomous as possible
- informing the treatment team of anything else that is happening in the family that may negatively impact your own recovery and the recovery of your relative.

Individual family counselling and family group work interventions (e.g., multifamily groups, psychoeducational groups, mutual support groups) can help people to develop coping strategies, identify risk factors that could point to someone having another episode, and support families during this stressful time. Many families find it helpful to meet with other families and report that they feel less isolated and alone when they hear that other families have gone through similar experiences. Families can also share their expertise and experiences with one another.

A parent writes:

*There is some form of learning or education that happens through talking with others about the facts of the illness and our experience with it. I know that I found strength from others. I cannot say enough about the value of the family support group at* LEARN *[Learning Employment Advocacy Recreation Network, a part of* CAMH*] and the amazing people who facilitate it. Here is a place where there are other people who truly know what we are going through, and it is a place where we can say what we really feel in a way that we might not with friends and family. Our challenges and frustrations are often common ones, and learning that helps us to feel less alone, along with learning how we might better deal with the issues facing us now and what may be ahead. The latter is a little scary for most of us, I think.*

## Siblings' concerns

Siblings often tell us that they feel confused by the illness. Here are some reactions that siblings have shared with us:

- Anger: "Why is my sibling getting so much attention from my family?"
- Resentment: "My sibling brought this illness on herself by using drugs and alcohol. My parents' lives revolve around my sibling's happiness. What about me?"
- Sadness and loss: "My sibling isn't the person that he used to be" and "My

family isn't what it used to be."

· Fear and anxiety: "Will I become ill myself?" "Will I always have to take care of my sibling?"

· Guilt: "How can I enjoy myself when my relative is so ill?" "Did I contribute to causing the psychosis?"

· Overcompensating: "I have to be the perfect child to make up for the difficulties my parents are having with my sibling."

· Taking on parental duties: "I will cook and do everything I can to look after my brother and sister."

· Denial: "I'm doing everything that I can to stay away from home, drinking, partying . . ."

Many siblings report that their parents are so focused on helping their relative with the illness that it feels like there is little time for them. These siblings feel ignored and left out of the family. Parents report that although they know that dedicating special time for each of their children is important, it is sometimes easier said than done. It is important for all family members to have the opportunity to talk about their feelings and experience and to learn more about psychosis. It is helpful to talk with other siblings who have been through similar experiences. Remind yourself to have patience: there are no magical solutions to helping your family members through this time.

Families new to Canada may face additional challenges. It is stressful to leave your country of origin and start again in a new country. Sometimes there is a reversal of roles between parents and children when the children can speak English or French better than their parents. Siblings who have had this experience write of the extra responsibilities and pressures on them in helping their parents navigate the new world that they find themselves in.

## LATER PHASES OF ILLNESS

Most families are able to move forward and, with time, continue to grow and flourish. Families develop expertise and coping skills and recognize that recovery is not a linear process. They learn how to cope with setbacks and challenges and nurture themselves during this process. Some family members may have coped well during the crisis period and may experience their own "crash" when their relative starts feeling better. Families vary in the challenges they may have experienced in the past and sometimes issues that came before the onset of psychosis will come to the surface. Challenges may involve a death in the family, mental health or addiction issues, migration, trauma, marital conflict, divorce and financial hardship. These issues may affect the way that you are coping with your relative's illness and can be detrimental to your own well-being. It is important to remember that you are not alone and that there is help available to you.

Here are one family's thoughts on their experience at this phase of the journey:

*And what about the future and hope? My son was a very bright young man, a little lost in the direction he was headed in life, but he had finished his OACs and I believed he would find his way. He had been living with friends and had been working and running his own affairs. He had quit one job and quickly lost another at the time he returned to live with me, just when the positive symptoms were becoming more apparent. In those early days, before and after medication, he needed to be taken care of like a much younger person, but we've moved toward a more adultlike relationship again as he has been getting stronger.*

*It has been an adjustment in so many ways, and I have had to monitor my own reactions and feelings as well as his, and to remember all the advice to also take care of myself. I want my son to be better, of course, and I grasp at any indication that he is making progress, which sometimes seems so little and so slow. I have come to realize that this is not going to be a straight path and that there will be ups and downs for him and therefore for me too. I had lost a big part of him for a while and it could happen again, but for now I see more of him returning, and more and more good days than bad, which wasn't the case not so many months ago. I remember when I heard him singing one day, and I knew that things were changing. He was able to hold some work for a short time again recently, which was a good milestone too, and the momentum is building. Someone recently said that none of us would be the same people we were before the first episode. I suppose time and elusive patience will reveal just what this means.*

# Stress reduction

When a person is initially diagnosed with psychosis, family members often experience emotions such as sorrow, anger, disbelief and denial. While this is normal, it can disturb the balance of family life in the short term. Family members need to give themselves time to readjust to their new reality.

We find that families often focus on supporting their relative and forget about supporting themselves. Family members need to find a balance between supporting their recovering relative and finding time for themselves. Many of you have told us that your well-being is directly linked to how your relative is doing. While this is natural, caregivers need to manage their own stress to effectively participate in their relative's recovery and provide sustainable support for all family members.

## HOW STRESSED ARE YOU?

How can you assess how stressed you are at any given point in time? How can you know if your stress levels have reached such a point that you may need to be referred to your family doctor or a psychiatrist for additional support and help?

Many of you may feel vulnerable and worried about the future. This is a normal reaction to the difficult situation that you find yourself in. You may notice a change in your productivity on the job and have difficulty handling your usual responsibilities. You may also be focusing more on the past than the future. Learning to recognize the signs of stress within yourself will help you avoid the burnout that can arise from coping with a family member with a mental illness. Speak to one of the team members or contact your local family doctor if you experience the following for more than two weeks:

· starting to feel as if you cannot "hold your life together"
· changes in eating and sleeping patterns
· inability to continue your job or other usual activities
· feeling pessimistic about the future
· lessened enjoyment and pleasure out of life
· excessive use of alcohol and/or other drugs
· withdrawal from your usual support system
· difficulty concentrating, remembering things and making decisions

- a sustained change in your personality, thinking and behaviour (as observed by you or others)
- thoughts or plans of ending your life.

In case of an emergency, for example, if you feel suicidal, go to the nearest emergency department. Remember, there is help available.

Filling in the Personal Stress Awareness Map in Appendix 7 will help family members understand how they are dealing with stress at any given moment. Try to be forgiving of yourself and remember that you will need to take care of yourself and reduce your own stress levels before you are able to take care of your relative and the rest of the family. Try to not allow the stresses of the illness to consume your entire life.

A family member writes:

> I had to learn to live in the moment and block all my fears and anxiety about the future to reduce my own stress levels.

## SUGGESTIONS FOR HOW CAREGIVERS CAN NURTURE THEMSELVES

We have compiled some tips from suggestions generated by participants in our groups to help family members nurture themselves. This is not meant to be a complete list. Taking care of yourself is a highly individual process. Remember which strategies have worked in the past. Some people experiencing psychosis have told us that it is reassuring for them when the rest of their family resumes their regular routines.

- Recognize your own symptoms of stress.
- Focus on your own feelings, needs and wants.
- Pay attention to your own physical and mental health and try to establish good routines for yourself.
- Cut down on alcohol, caffeine, sugar, fats and tobacco. These substances can put a strain on your body's ability to cope with stress.
- Remember to eat regularly and eat a varied, healthy diet. Eating a balanced diet will enhance your physical and mental health.
- Try to get a good night's sleep and exercise on a regular basis. If you have difficulty falling asleep, try to practise relaxation exercises on a regular basis.
- If you are able to do so, make changes in your work or family situation (e.g., schedule, workload, household duties).

- Do the essential tasks and prioritize the rest. Maintaining balance in your life will help counteract the stresses that you are experiencing.
- Try to give yourself the time and space to move through this difficult time in your life. Treat yourself with the same compassion and respect as you would someone else in your life.
- Establish a routine for yourself.
- Keep busy. This helps you stop ruminating about your situation.
- Maintain or establish a good support system for yourself:
  - Try to avoid becoming isolated.
  - Get the help that you need to sustain you at this time.
  - Reach out to others. Choose people whom you can talk to. Stay away from those who emphasize the negative. Remember, not everyone can empathize with your predicament or can offer support.
  - If you have a partner, try to spend some quality time nurturing this relationship.
  - Talk with clergy, doctors and/or professional counsellors about the things that are bothering you.
- Psychoeducational and mutual aid support groups can be helpful. Groups can make you feel less socially isolated. You may find that many other people share your issues. Remember that knowledge is power.
- You can change your own thoughts, attitudes and behaviour, but remember that you do not have the power to change anyone else except yourself.
- Remember that you are not to blame for the illness. You cannot always control everything that is happening around you, but you can learn how to change your response to the stressor or situation.

  A caregiver writes:

  > Learn to take a step back and separate yourself a little from your loved one. When things get difficult, it can help to view your child as you would view a troubled friend. How would you talk to someone unrelated to you, in that situation? This is **not** easy, but it is important to try to differentiate between caring about the other person and taking responsibility for the other person. Sometimes you can just provide guidance and advice. You don't always have to take all the responsibility for solving problems onto your own shoulders.

- Cultivate interests outside the family that are not connected with mental health problems. Continue your involvement with activities away from home. This will help prevent you from feeling a loss of identity.

- Stress can be relieved through exercise such as cycling, joining a gym and other sports. It can also be relieved through gardening, hobbies, going to movies or doing other activities you enjoy.
- Taking time for yourself on a regular basis can help you approach your situation with more control and will enable you to pace yourself and maintain your energy.
- Remember that it is important to "let go of control" and be able to detach from your situation. Adaptive denial (deliberately working on an optimistic outlook and filling your thoughts with day-to-day details about things *other than* your loved one's situation) can be important in helping you to feel centred.
- Remember that you can work off your anger through physical activity.
- Pay attention to your emotional needs. Visit friends, read, start a journal, cultivate a hobby, listen to music, dance, enjoy your pet.
- Remember the importance of humour and permit yourself to have fun with the people you enjoy. You are entitled to laugh and find joy in your life.
- Nature can revive you. A family member writes, "the birds at my feeder, the wind in the trees, the garden restore my spirits."
- Get respite when needed and remind yourself that nobody can be on call 24/7. If you are able to go away on a trip or holiday, do so. Plan regular times to recharge your batteries. Remember that you are also important and need to nurture yourself and devote some special time to yourself each day. Have a massage, a cup of tea or a bubble bath.
- Families have suggested that regular meditation, relaxation exercises, yoga, tai chi and prayer can be helpful. Some of you have strong ties to your places of worship. Others achieve a sense of inner peace by being in nature. Do whatever works for you.
- Hope and faith can be important factors in helping you cope with the day-to-day struggles.
- Try to create a low-stress environment in your family.
- Try to remember that negative feelings are normal and give yourself permission to feel angry toward your relative or your situation in general.

A mother shares:

> *You are entitled to your feelings. You may feel frustrated, angry, confused, upset or depressed at times, but this is okay! Remember you are in the emotional Olympics and it is very difficult. Try to be*

*accepting and forgiving toward yourself. Talk about your emotions with a trusted friend, family member or professional. Working through your emotions helps let them go. It is normal to feel fearful and anxious about the future. Try and live in the here and now and proceed one step at a time.*

· Set limits. Forgive yourself when you have trouble sticking to your plan and try to start all over again. Remember you are not perfect and are doing the best job you can do.
· Remember that your stress level will lower as your coping improves. Remind yourself that recovery is a process and if your relative cannot do something today, this does not mean that he or she will be unable to do this thing in the future.
· Try to separate the person from the illness and appreciate and accept your relative as he or she is in the present.
· Try to focus on your relative's strengths and positive qualities rather than emphasizing your relative's problems. There will be improvements and setbacks. It is important not to put too much emphasis on either one.
· Keep a journal of emotional or stressful states and start to identify positive ways that you are dealing with your stress.
· Try to focus on your own strengths and positive qualities.
· Consider doing volunteer work: this can help you feel better about your own situation.
· Try to balance your life between your relative, work, spiritual, recreational and social pursuits, not necessarily in this order.

Change occurs slowly. You may be surprised how much better and stronger you start to feel once you make a small change in your self-care routine.

# Communication

It is best not to take your ill relative's angry or hurtful words to heart when he or she is not well. Learning how to become assertive is a skill and—like any other skill—it takes time and practice to improve your ability to communicate more effectively. When you model assertive behaviour, your relative and the rest of the family may also develop assertiveness and adaptive communication skills.

Our colleagues, April Collins and Dr. Gary Remington, have permitted us to print the following piece on communication from *Learning about Schizophrenia*, published in 1999, CAMH, Toronto.

> *Even at the best of times, problems arise in all families. However, when people are struggling to cope with a mental illness like psychosis, communication can easily get frustrating and strained. It is for this reason that we recommend that all families set aside some time to regularly review the features of good communication. This will hopefully help lower the tension and defuse conflicts in the family should they arise. There is some evidence in the literature that suggests that improving communication skills may reduce the likelihood of relapse in persons with psychosis. It's important to keep in mind that accepting that conflictual communication can increase a person's risk for relapse does not mean that family members should walk on eggshells or avoid raising questions or concerns. It means that for everyone involved attacking, belittling, or criticism is not helpful at any time. Instead, negative feelings should be expressed directly and constructively.*

## How is communication affected?

> *For the person with the illness, psychosis creates some unique problems with respect to communication. Some of the symptoms can interfere with the ability to communicate clearly with friends and family. These include:*
> - *Confusion resulting from the inability to separate real from unreal events when one is still experiencing symptoms.*
> - *Problems concentrating, and paying attention to what other people are saying, getting distracted or lost in his or her own thoughts. This can happen a lot if he or she is hearing voices.*
> - *Problems organizing thoughts and getting ideas across to other people.*
> - *Flat affect (the person's face shows little or no emotional expression, so it's hard to tell how the person is feeling).*

## HOW DOES ALL OF THIS IMPACT ON THE FAMILY?

*For the family, the stress of coping with the ill person's illness often can, at times, leave family members feeling tired and on edge. This is not the time for the family to tackle major issues, if possible. Because the stress levels are often very high, discussions that occur at these times are inclined to produce less than satisfactory results because often things are said in the heat of the moment that may not be easily forgotten or forgiven. As such, it is important to postpone the discussion of serious or tough issues until the ill person is feeling settled.*

Reprinted with permission of the authors.

Here are some excellent suggestions offered by Kim Mueser and Susan Gingerich (1994) to help families communicate effectively with their ill relative:

1. Get to the point. The ill person may have difficulty focusing/following a discussion; therefore get to the point quickly. This can be done by:
   - clearly stating the topic or concern
   - using direct, simple language
   - keeping the message brief and low key.
2. Express feelings directly—one way of being clear about your feelings is to use "I" statements:
   - speak directly to the person and accept responsibility for what you say
   - make a verbal "feeling" statement (e.g., "I get worried when you come home late")
   - speak in a calm, clear voice
   - don't assume your relative will know how you feel if you don't tell him/her
   - express your feelings directly, when problems occur—don't wait until later unless you cannot be calm.
3. Use praise and make positive requests:
   - make eye contact/look at the person
   - smile
   - tell him or her in a warm tone what specifically he or she did that pleased you
   - use an "I" statement to say how it makes you feel (e.g., "Thanks; I really appreciated it when you took out the garbage").
4. Check out what the other person thinks—rather than guessing what your

relative is thinking or feeling, listen carefully to what is being said, ask questions when you don't understand or something is unclear and check out what you have heard.

- Listen carefully.
- Let people speak for themselves.
- Ask questions when you don't understand.
- Repeat back what you've heard and ask if that is what your relative meant.
- Ask more questions if necessary.
- Be clear and specific.
- Avoid long sentences and introductions to topics.
- Focus on behaviours, not attitudes or personality traits.
- Make direct requests that specify exactly what you would like; concentrate on one topic at a time.

Reproduced with permission from Mueser, K.T. and Gingerich, S. (1994). *Coping with Schizophrenia: A Guide for Families*. Oakland, CA: New Harbinger Publications.

# Setting limits

Setting limits and defining clear boundaries between people is important in all healthy relationships. People with psychosis cannot differentiate between what is reality and what is not. Setting firm and consistent definitions of unacceptable behaviour is imperative for the well-being and safety of everyone in the family. Having clear boundaries can provide a structured, predictable and secure environment for your relative.

TIPS: **Some suggestions for setting limits**
Many of you have told us that you feel at a loss in setting limits with your ill relative. The following suggestions are often helpful for families when issues regarding setting limits on behaviour arise:
· Have patience.
· Try to accept and embrace your relative in the here and now.
· Take the lead from your relative with psychosis.
· Try to understand your relative's need to withdraw from the family when he or she feels overstimulated and needs some quiet time to calm down.
· Set boundaries about what is and is not permissible in the home.

- Set limits in a calm, matter-of-fact fashion.
- Be prepared to ensure that your relative complies with the limits set.
- If your relative does not conform to the agreed-upon rules, try to be consistent in following through with set consequences and appropriate action.
- Communicate with your parenting partner and try to be consistent with one another in setting limits.

## WHAT BEHAVIOUR IS UNACCEPTABLE?

Each family is unique and may have a varying tolerance of certain behaviours. However, it is important for you to pay attention to, accept and respect your own feelings, especially if you feel intimidated or concerned about your relative's behaviour.

The following behaviours are unacceptable:
- Physical aggression such as pushing, grabbing or pinching.
- Clear emotional abuse, such as yelling profanity or verbally aggressive threats.
- Sexual abuse.
- Property damage, such as damaging furniture or cars.
- Setting fires or creating fire hazards, such as smoking in bed.
- Stealing from family, friends or others.
- Using non-prescribed drugs or alcohol, which complicate the psychiatric disorder.
- Financial mismanagement, such as engaging in spending sprees.
- Severely disruptive or tyrannical behaviours, such as insisting that all family members eat only certain foods, refusing to let anyone use the phone or barricading the doors. (Bartha et al., 2001)

Reproduced with permission from Bartha, C., Kitchen, K., Parker, C., Thomson, C. (2001). *Depression & Bipolar Disorder Family Psychoeducational Group Manual: Therapist Guide.* Toronto: Centre for Addiction and Mental Health.

As a general rule, it is not helpful to allow your relatives to do something that will be harmful to themselves or others. When in doubt, discuss your concerns with a friend or member of the professional team. Some family members have told us that they have been living in chaos for such a long time that they need someone else to do a reality check with them and determine whether a behaviour is acceptable or unacceptable. They say they have started to "adjust to a new reality of what is normal." (See Appendix 5 for suggestions on establishing/setting your own boundaries.)

# DO OTHER FAMILIES FIND IT DIFFICULT TO SET LIMITS?

Many parents have told us that they feel disempowered when dealing with an adult child who may be acting out at home or intentionally breaking the family rules. You need to remember that you do have leverage over your children, particularly if your relative is living in the family home. It is your right to determine the family boundaries and ensure that your relative accepts the limits in your family home. This may involve asserting the family's right to feel secure and comfortable in their own home. Many of you might think that if you ignore negative behaviour, it will disappear on its own. This is not the case. Sometimes, things have to go from bad to worse before people realize that they need to step in and take some control over the situation.

Setting limits can be very difficult, particularly if rules and discipline have been relaxed in the past. However, it is necessary for those of you who are parents to contain unsafe or destructive behaviour.

A parent writes:

*I let my child with psychosis behave in an abusive way to myself, and the rest of my children took the lead from their sibling and copied this behaviour. It was at this stage that I realized that I had to take charge of the situation and separate the illness from my child's personality and let my child know that this type of behaviour is not acceptable in my household. Life settled down for the better after this time.*

Another caregiver writes about setting up regular chores and rules around the house for her relative:

*I felt odd about setting up a schedule for my relative. I had done this with her when she was a much younger child and I felt as if I was minimizing her as an adult by reinforcing the basic rules about the house. She seemed to thrive on the structure and, in time, I could back off as she gradually started to take more responsibility for her own self-care and set about doing some chores around the house. It is difficult to negotiate between my child's need for independence and her dependence on me. Having other parents who have been in similar predicaments to my own has been helpful in encouraging me to stay the course."*

## The importance of families setting limits on themselves

It is important to set limits for yourself so that you don't become consumed by your relative's illness (see the section "Suggestions for how caregivers can nurture themselves," page 43). Having an ill relative can exert a lot of strain on all relationships within the family.

Take time to schedule regular dates with your partner to sustain the relationship.

Agree not to speak about your fears and worries about your relative with significant others before you go to sleep.

Maintain regular family routines.

# Hope for the future: tapping into your resilience

It is important to have hope for your own and your relatives' recovery.

The recovery process for your relative and yourself may take longer than you had initially expected and there may be times when you feel impatient and hopeless about the future. Hope involves believing in your own ability to overcome adversity and "bounce back" into life. Countless families have demonstrated their resilience in living with their relative recovering from psychosis. Resilience is the ability to withstand and prevail over adverse life circumstances.

## EVERY CLOUD CAN HAVE A SILVER LINING

Although we know that the stress of dealing with illness can challenge the family's ability to stay together, some of you have reminded us that while weathering a crisis involves facing danger, it also presents an opportunity to break down existing patterns and establish new patterns for yourself. In the words of one caregiver, many families manage to deal with the "turbulence" in their midst by "riding the wave and going on to reach calmer waters." Other family members have described the experience of dealing with psychosis as a catalyst for positive change in the family in ways that they could never have imagined.

Some of you have described a new sense of closeness with your relative with psychosis and with the rest of your family, and achieving a different appreciation for life as you and your relative travel on the road to recovery.

# THERE IS A LIGHT AT THE END OF THE TUNNEL

*There Is a Light at the End of the Tunnel* is an accounting of the journey of two sisters during the first year of their brother's treatment for psychosis. It addresses the notion of the treatment team and family members having hope when the sisters felt despondent and without hope for their brother's future. They describe so well how the illness robbed them of the brother they once knew, and what the road was like on the way to their brother's recovery. Their narrative demonstrates that siblings very often go through their own readjustment and pain brought on by the stresses of living with someone with psychosis.

*Some memories are haunting, we would rather forget them, but they are not forgettable. We can still recall the times when we tried hard to bring a smile to our faces. We call our family a united family—us two sisters and our one and only brother. No one sees us as siblings, but as best friends. We always have something to do together, something to talk about and laugh about. As older sisters, we are fond of our brother —the youngest in our family.*

*But suddenly, his closeness toward us started to disappear, his behaviour and character started to change. He started to get angry for no apparent reason; he didn't talk to anyone or listen to anyone anymore. His grades started to drop at high school and he finally dropped out of school altogether. He was no longer our fun-loving, caring brother, but a total stranger to us. He was no longer a funny guy, but very reserved. No longer caring, but aggressive and violent. No longer did we have sweet, carefree talks. Instead, he was verbally very abusive.*

*He seemed to be in his own world. We wondered, what's wrong with him? Is anything bothering him? Why doesn't he talk about it? Why doesn't he bother about his appearance or take care of himself? Why is he living like a dead person? Why doesn't he understand that we are always there for him no matter what happens? Where is our brother who carried a big, heavy fish tank by bus to give it to one of us for our birthday as a surprise gift? What can we do to get our brother back? We asked these questions every single day, every hour and every minute.*

*Our lives started to change too. Tensions, depression. We did not know what would be the breaking news at our home when we came home from school or work. We didn't know how many more times we would have to go to our brother and plead with him to tell us what was bothering him. Nothing worked out. But the only thing we had in our mind was, no matter what happens, he is our brother, we have to help him and he needs our help. But how to do this? He was 19 years old, an adult. Only he could choose what he wanted.*

*The problem did not stop here. Conflict between our mom and dad started to increase. Dad started to blame mom and us for our brother's behaviour. The problems started to pile up every day and we felt trapped between all of these problems. We had to stop dad and mom, or dad and brother from fighting. Finally, my parents separated. With God's help, my brother was admitted to* CAMH. *My brother got his life back from this time on. The doctor and social workers helped us so much. His social worker on the unit was amazing and he helped us to make our life bright again. With this worker's help, we had a chance to meet a wonderful and always cheerful family worker. We went to her family meetings and at the time there was a girl who said that, "there is always a light at the end of the tunnel." At that time, we didn't believe in these words and thought that our life was always going to be stuck in the tunnel.*

*When your life is on the bumpy road, you don't believe in miracles.*

*But the miracle came into our life. With doctors, social workers and the medications' help, my brother is doing excellently within one year of treatment. We have our "old brother" back again. Before he was a chain smoker, now he quit smoking and is doing volunteer work. He is taking boxing and will continue his studies very soon. There were times when we just sat and stared at the window with tears rolling down our faces without our permission. Only our pillowcases and the washroom mirror know the pain and the sorrow we have faced in our lives. But now, when we look at the mirror, we see happy faces, smiling slowly, full of hope in our life and hopeful about our brother's life. We are out of the tunnel and have seen the bright light in our life.*

# Final words

A sibling writes:

*When P was in the hospital, we put everything on hold—school, our work, our social lives. It was all for P, but we needed to do it for ourselves, too, to try to start a family healthy from the start. (Ptasznik, A., 2007–08)*

She continues:

*Today, we are able to look back and see P's illness as a silver lining. We know that no matter how bad the situation may be at times, something positive will result and we will come out strong. (CAMH Foundation Annual Report, 2006–2007)*

It is our hope that this guide will be helpful to you as you work as an ally in your relative's recovery. We also hope that this guide will be a resource for your own recovery as a family member. Remember that while no one knows what the future holds for your ill relative, the best outcomes will be achieved when you work together with your relative and the treatment team to emphasize the protective factors and strengths in you and your relative and minimize the risk factors as much as you can.

# References

Bartha, C., Kitchen, K., Parker, C. & Thomson, C. (2001). *Depression and Bipolar Disorder Family Psychoeducation Group Manual.* Toronto: Centre for Addiction and Mental Health.

Lehman, A. & Steinwachs, D.M. (1998). Patterns of usual care for schizophrenia: Initial results from the schizophrenia patient outcomes research team (PORT) client survey. *Schizophrenia Bulletin, 24* (1), 11–20.

Meuser, K. & Gingerich, S. (1994). *Coping with Schizophrenia: A Guide for Families.* Oakland, CA: New Harbinger.

Ptasznik, A. (2007–08). Double Whammy: When early psychosis and substance use go hand in hand. *CrossCurrents, 11* (2), 9–11.

O'Grady, C.P. & Skinner, W.J.W. (2007). *A Family Guide to Concurrent Disorders.* Toronto: Centre for Addiction and Mental Health.

Remington, G. & Collins, A. (1999). *Learning about Schizophrenia.* Toronto: Centre for Addiction and Mental Health.

Schizophrenia Society of Canada. (2003). *Learning about Schizophrenia: Rays of Hope; A Reference Manual for Families and Caregivers* (3rd Rev. ed.). Markham, ON: Author.

# Glossary of terms

**abstinence**. Complete avoidance of using a substance or substances.

**against medical advice (AMA)**. Whereby a voluntary patient decides to do something (e.g., leave hospital) against the recommendation of his or her physician.

**antipsychotic** (also **neuroleptic** or **psychotropic**). A medication created to treat the symptoms of psychosis. Antipsychotics are categorized as atypicals (newer) medications or as typical or conventional (older) medications.

**case manager**. The main person in the clinical case management model for delivering and co-ordinating services for your relative. He or she will assess your relative's needs on an ongoing basis and provide the necessary services to meet these needs. The case manager also co-ordinates with the rest of the treatment team.

**clozapine**. An antipsychotic medication that is only used when two or more other antipsychotic medications have not worked. Its use is closely monitored because it has a side-effect of lowering white blood cell counts, which can be dangerous.

**cognitive-behavioural therapy (CBT)**. A form of psychotherapy that focuses on the thought and behaviour patterns of the individual. CBT can be done in an individual or group format.

**computerized axial tomography (CAT) scan**. A method of diagnosis employing X-rays taken from different angles and then analyzed by computer to produce a representation of the part of the body in crosssection.

**confidentiality**. A principle observed by most professionals that dictates that the information and activities in the professional relationship are kept private.

**consent**. Permission; to give permission.

**Consent and Capacity Board** (often **Review Board**). An independent tribunal affiliated with the Ministry of Health and Long-Term Care. The Board sits in panels of one, three or five members. It hears and decides cases under the Mental Health Act, the Substitute Decisions Act, the Health Care Consent Act and the Long-Term Care Act. The most common cases involve involuntary committal to hospital and cases pertaining to clients' incapacity to make treatment decisions.

**harm reduction**. Reducing the harmful effects of alcohol or other drugs without expecting abstinence.

**incapable**. A medical assessment made by the client's doctor that the client is unable to make treatment decisions for himself or herself, manage his or her own finances or disclose his or her own private medical information. People are deemed incapable of making treatment decisions for themselves when they are unable to comprehend that they have an illness, and/or don't understand the benefits and costs of accepting or refusing treatment.

**inpatient**. A person who stays in a hospital while receiving treatment.

**insight-oriented therapies**. Psychotherapies that focus on the role of conscious and unconscious motivations, drives and conflicts that play a role in the development of mental disorders.

**interdisciplinary team** (also **multidisciplinary team**). A group of medical staff from different disciplines (e.g., psychiatry, nursing and allied professions such as social work and occupational therapy) who work as a team to provide assessment and treatment services.

**involuntary patient**. A person forced to stay in hospital when a psychiatrist deems that he or she would otherwise pose a risk to himself or herself or to the community. Being made an involuntary patient is also known as being **certified**. Patients can appeal their certification or involuntary status. Criteria for involuntary committal include posing a danger to self, posing a danger to others and inability to care for oneself.

**Justice of the Peace** (**JP**). A provincial judicial officer who tries cases involving infractions of municipal bylaws, issues warrants for arrest, administers oaths, and so on. A JP can also issue a Form 2, which requires a person to be brought to a hospital for a risk assessment and evaluation.

**magnetic resonance imaging** (**MRI**) **scan**. A process of producing images of the body by means of a strong magnetic field and low energy radio waves.

**Mental Health Act**. An Ontario provincial law governing mental health practice. Legislation varies from province to province.

**negative symptoms**. Expected behaviours that are missing (e.g., lack of full range of emotions [flat affect], lack of motivation, inability to feel pleasure in previously enjoyed activities, social withdrawal).

**outpatient**. A person who receives treatment while residing in the community.

**Parkinsonian symptoms**. A cluster of symptoms similar to those seen in Parkinson's disease. Symptoms include shuffling gait, decreased energy, decreased or absent body activity, masklike facial expression and variable tremor.

**perception**. Information gathered through the senses (hearing, vision, smell, taste and touch); the act of gathering information in this way.

**positive symptoms**. Behavioural abnormalities that are unexpected (e.g., hearing voices, fixed false beliefs, bizarre behaviour).

**psychoeducation**. Non-medical interventions designed to optimize functioning and recovery; includes psychotherapy and education about the illness and recovery.

**psychosis**. Any serious mental disorder in which a person loses touch with reality. Common symptoms include hallucinations, delusions and disorganized thinking.

**psychosocial rehabilitation**. Non-biological interventions that focus on other determinants of mental health (e.g., psychological, vocational, relational, spiritual, social, environmental, recreational).

**psychotherapy** (also **talk therapy**). The treatment of mental disorders through interaction with a therapist. There are many different types of psychotherapy (e.g., supportive, psychoanalytic, cognitive-behavioural). The therapist can be a doctor, psychologist, social worker, nurse or other health care professional.

**recovery**. The resolution of symptoms over time (with or without therapy) and the return to "normal" functioning. The length of recovery varies from person to person.

**rehabilitation**. Therapy to restore a person to his or her previous level of functioning.

**relapse**. A return of symptoms, or, if still present, a worsening of symptoms.

**rights advisor**. A person who provides information to psychiatric clients about their rights regarding decisions made by their physician (e.g., concerning admission to hospital and capacity issues).

**stigma.** Shame and disgrace resulting in social isolation and discrimination.

**substance abuse.** Use of psychoactive drugs (including alcohol) in a way that poses significant hazards to health and interferes with social, occupational, psychological or physical functioning.

**substitute decision-maker (SDM).** A person authorized to make decisions on behalf of someone deemed "incapable."

**tardive dyskinesia.** Uncoordinated involuntary movements of the face, tongue and hands.

**vocation.** An occupation, profession or trade.

**voluntary patient.** A person who freely chooses to be admitted or remain in hospital for assessment and treatment. Such a patient does not meet the criteria for involuntary committal. Voluntary patients can leave the hospital at any time.

# Educational resources

## EDUCATION

### Books

Adamec, C. (1996). *How to Live with a Mentally Ill Person: A Handbook of Day-to-Day Strategies.* New York: John Wiley & Sons.

Amador, X. (2000). *I Am Not Sick: I Don't Need Help!* Peconic, NY: Vida Press.

Andreasen, N. (1984). *The Broken Brain.* New York: Harper and Row.

Canadian Mental Health Association. (2005). *A Sibling's Guide to Psychosis.* Toronto: Author.

Czuchta, D. & Ryan, K. (1999). *First Episode Psychosis: An Information Guide.* Toronto: Centre for Addiction and Mental Health.

De Hert, M., Magiels, G. & Thys, E. (2003). *The Secret of the Brain Chip.* Antwerp, Belgium: EPO.

Hyde, M. (1996). *Know about Mental Illness.* New York: Walker & Company.

Schizophrenia Society of Ontario. (2003). *Learning about Schizophrenia: Rays of Hope; A Reference Manual for Families and Caregivers* (3rd Rev. ed.). Markham, ON: Author.

Woolis, R. (1992). *When Someone You Love Has a Mental Illness: A Handbook for Family, Friends and Caregivers*. New York: Tarcher/Perigee.

## Videos

**Working Together: Things Can Get Better** (London: London Health Sciences Centre, 180 minutes)

A three-part series designed for families of people with psychosis. The video explains the basics of psychosis, including symptoms, the need for early intervention, treatment and the recovery process. The video shares the perspectives of clients, families and mental health care professionals.

**One Day at a Time** (Canadian Mental Health Association, 28 minutes)

Several members of a first episode psychosis support group describe their experiences as parents of young people with psychosis. The video was developed to provide information and support to parents new to the experience of psychosis in their family—from other parents who have had similar experiences.

**Changing Minds** (CTV, W-FIVE presentation, 20 minutes)

A presentation about young people with schizophrenia, in which two young people diagnosed with schizophrenia—Simon and Tara—and their families are interviewed about their experience with the illness, treatment and recovery.

**First Break** (National Film Board of Canada, 51 minutes)

This video explores the different outcomes of a first episode of mental illness on three young adults and their families. Filmed over a year, the video dispels myths around mental illness, and questions the stigma associated with it, while providing a powerful portrait of coping.

**The Myths of Mental Illness** (National Film Board of Canada, 56 minutes)

This video tells the story of a successful journalist, his breakdown and his battle to regain his life's meaning after suffering from a mental illness. The film raises questions about coping with stressful life and work situations, mental health and illness, psychiatry, drug therapy and psychotherapy, the healing power of human relationships, human freedom and dignity, technology and the invasion of privacy, and media integrity.

## Websites

**Canadian Mental Health Association, Early Psychosis Intervention Project,**
National Office, Toronto, Ontario
www.cmha.ca

**Early Psychosis Intervention (EPI) Program,** Fraser Health Authority,
British Columbia
www.psychosissucks.ca

**Early Psychosis Treatment Service (EPTS),** Alberta Health Services
www.calgaryhealthregion.ca/mh/EPTP/epp

**Early Psychosis Intervention (EPI) Youth and Family Education Initiative**
www.gethelpearly.ca

**Early Psychosis Prevention and Intervention Centre (EPPIC),** Australia
www.eppic.org.au

**Get on Top: A Guide to Mental Health,** The Compass Strategy, Australia
www.getontop.org

**Open the Doors, World Psychiatric Association**
www.openthedoors.com

**Peer Support for Parents of Psychosis Sufferers (PSPOPS)**
www.psychosissupport.com

**Prevention and Early Intervention Program for Psychoses (PEPP)**
London, Ontario
www.pepp.ca

**Rethink**
www.rethink.org

**Schizophrenia Society of Ontario**
www.schizophrenia.ca

**SSO Youth Awareness Program, Schizophrenia Society of Ontario**
www.ssoaware.com

# Tracking early signs of relapse

An important part of relapse prevention is the ability to identify early warning signs of your relative's illness. Some of these early signs you can observe, while other signs are more subjective and known only to the ill relative. It may be helpful to identify the early signs you have noticed and if your ill relative is able, list the subjective symptoms he or she experiences early in the illness. Hint: focus on behaviour you observe, emotional expressions shown and reported to you, things that are said, etc.

List the signs you have noticed in the space below.

_____
_____
_____
_____
_____
_____
_____
_____
_____
_____
_____
_____
_____
_____

# APPENDIX 4

# Creating a crisis card

People with mental health problems and their family members have found it extremely helpful to write important information on a card or a piece of paper folded small enough so that it can be carried with them wherever they go. For example, the card or paper may be placed in a visible part of the person's wallet.

A crisis card usually contains information important for others (e.g., friends, health care workers, police, strangers) to have in the event that your relative experiences a mental health–related crisis while away from home.

Here are some suggestions for information that you might include on a crisis card. Choose the information that would be most useful in your situation.

Reproduced with permission from O'Grady, C.P., Skinner, W.J.W. (2007). *A Family Guide to Concurrent Disorders*. Toronto: Centre for Addiction and Mental Health.

## EMERGENCY PERSONAL CONTACTS

**Primary contact** _____

Name _____ Home phone # _____

Work phone # _____ Cellphone # _____

E-mail _____

**Back-up contact** _____

Name _____ Home phone # _____

Work phone # _____ Cellphone # _____

E-mail _____

## TREATMENT PROVIDERS

**Family doctor** _____

Name _____

Phone # _____

**Case manager / therapist / substance use or mental health worker**

Name _____ Phone # _____

Name _____ Phone # _____

**Hospital or treatment centre** _____

Name _____ Phone # _____


## CURRENT MEDICATIONS

Medication _____ Dose _____ Time of day _____

Medication allergies: _____

_____

_____

The following medications were ineffective and/or caused serious side-effects:

Medication _____ Side-effects _____

Suggestions for helping in a crisis or an emergency:

_____

_____

_____

_____

_____

_____

_____

# Setting loving boundaries

## The behaviour of your relative with psychosis:

What is my bottom line? What am I willing (not willing) to tolerate?

_____
_____
_____
_____

What are his or her responsibilities?

_____
_____
_____
_____

What are my responsibilities?

_____
_____
_____
_____

What are some ways that I can support my relative in his or her recovery?

_____

_____

_____

_____

# APPENDIX 6

# Hopefulness

We would like you to think about how hopeful you are about your own life. Please answer the following questions:

On a scale from one to 10, where would you place yourself today?

1      2      3      4      5      6      7      8      9      10

(Not at all hopeful)                    (Completely optimistic)

How does this compare with where you would have placed yourself when you started this group?

1      2      3      4      5      6      7      8      9      10

(Not at all hopeful)                    (Completely optimistic)

What were some of the things that helped your improvement?

_____

_____

_____

_____

What do you need to move up one more level?

_____

_____

_____

# APPENDIX 7

# Personal stress awareness map

Instructions:
· Check items that have applied to you over the past month.
· Underline or circle the top two to three symptoms, in each section, that disturb you the most.
· You might want to make photocopies of this page so other family members can take the test, and so you can take it again as you move along the path to your loved one's recovery, and see how your own recovery is going.

| EMOTIONAL | RELATIONSHIP | HABITS |
| --- | --- | --- |
| q frustration | q blame others | q smoking |
| q the blues | q intolerant | q using substances |
| q mood swings | q resentful | q drinking coffee, tea, soft drinks— to pick me up |
| q bad temper | q withdrawn | |
| q nightmares | q nagging | q drinking alcohol |
| q crying spells | q lonely | q biting fingernails |
| q irritable | q hiding | q often oversleeping |
| q worrying | q distrust | q taking uppers or downers |
| q no confidence | q explosive | q eating sugary foods—to pick me up |
| q no motivation | q critical of others | q constant eating—to pick me up |
| q feel depressed | q demanding | q rushing—constantly busy |
| q feel no one cares | | |
| q easily distracted | | |

| COGNITIVE SYSTEM | PERIPHERAL NERVOUS SYSTEM (Muscles) | AUTONOMIC NERVOUS SYSTEM (Organs, glands, vascular) |
|---|---|---|
| q forgetful | q tension headaches | q migraine headaches |
| q dull senses | q fatigue | q cold hands, feet |
| q no concentration | q low back pain | q appetite change |
| q low productivity | q muscle spasms | q stomach upset |
| q no creativity | q teeth-grinding | q loose bowels |
| q negative attitude | q breath-holding | q constipation |
| q confusion | q restlessness | q shallow breathing |
| q lethargy | q foot-tapping | q pounding heart |
| q whirling mind | q finger-drumming | q weight change |
| q boredom | q trouble sleeping | q many colds/flu |
| q blank mind | | q no sex drive |
| q no sense of humour | | q accident prone |
| | | q ulcers |
| | | q skin rashes, hives, psoriasis, dermatitis |

Many families have informed us that filling in this stress map has made them aware of the many ways that stress may impact all aspects of their life. If you have ticked off most of the items that have been listed, this would be a good time to speak to your family doctor and ensure that you receive the help you may need to help you get through this difficult time in your life. Other family members have informed us that this stress map has facilitated them becoming aware that they have "weathered a storm" and stress is no longer debilitating their general functioning.